T0128808

FULLNESS *of* TIME

FULLNESS *of* TIME

In His Perfect Time
My Testimony of A Spiritual Journey

Princess Delight

FULLNESS OF TIME
IN HIS PERFECT TIME MY TESTIMONY OF A SPIRITUAL JOURNEY

iUniverse books may be ordered through booksellers or by contacting:

iUniverse
1663 Liberty Drive
Bloomington, IN 47403
www.iuniverse.com
1-800-Authors (1-800-288-4677)

Because of the dynamic nature of the Internet, any web addresses or links contained in this book may have changed since publication and may no longer be valid. The views expressed in this work are solely those of the author and do not necessarily reflect the views of the publisher, and the publisher hereby disclaims any responsibility for them.

Any people depicted in stock imagery provided by Thinkstock are models, and such images are being used for illustrative purposes only. Certain stock imagery © Thinkstock.

ISBN: 978-1-5320-0550-3 (sc)
ISBN: 978-1-5320-0551-0 (e)

Library of Congress Control Number: 2016913736

Print information available on the last page.

iUniverse rev. date: 08/30/2016

To my Sovereign God who sits on the throne. You see all, and You know all. You are our all in all. All glory and honor to your holy name.

To my high school English teacher, Ms. Bernadette Ashby. You have been an inspiration to me—and the class of 1973. Thank you for your wisdom and your teaching.

To my reading audience—one or many—may you receive a word and a special touch from the Lord. He lives. I know my Redeemer lives!

In memory of my beloved parents who passed on their strong faith in God. Thank you! May our children and their children's children inherit this faith so that it will be passed on to future generations. Peace and love.

Contents

Acknowledgments ix

Introduction xi

Chapter 1   Testimony/Transparency/Truth 1

Chapter 2   Relationship/Response/Revelation 19

Chapter 3   Ultimate Silence/Unspoken
            Words/Until Now 34

Chapter 4   Calamity/Christ's Calling/Complete
            Closure 38

Chapter 5   Exposure/End-All/Eternity 52

Conclusion 65

Acknowledgments

My sisters Mercy, Marilyn, Mary, Liz, Shirley, Jemma, Angie, Anne, Wendy, and Charmaine. You have all stood by me in this season of testing. I call you my "sheroes." May you all continue to be a source of encouragement and inspiration.

My brothers Michael, David, Matthew, Mark, Joshua, Mervyn, Curtis, Gerard, and John. Whenever I called on you, you were there. Thank you for your support. Stay strong and stay blessed!

My friends Adrian, Sharon, Gloria, Kenny, Maria, Andrea, Ama, Dolorese and Barbara. You listened and offered me your prayers and kind words. Thank you all!

My sister-in-law, Marilyn, you were always on the lookout for me, especially on holidays and Costco Fridays. Thank you.

Pastor Phyllis, my adopted daughter, Donna and Ava. Thank you for your enthusiasm.

And, finally, to my calm, patient, and loving husband, Decell, my four gifted sons, Mel, Rel, Ron, and Vauhn, and my five talented grandchildren. You have all tolerated my many nights of not cooking without grumbling or murmuring while I was preoccupied with this book. Your support and encouragement have been priceless. You helped carry me through this experience in a way

I could never have imagined. I am truly grateful to each of you. I could not have accomplished this without your assistance.

God is great and greatly to be praised. "When we delight ourselves in Him, He will grant us the desires of our heart" (Ps. 37:4). His word is true, if we just believe! Pastor R. Cook always ended his devotions by saying, "Walk with the King and be a blessing!" Grace and peace.

Introduction

It was all a big setup, orchestrated by God for His purpose and His glory. I am now totally convinced that our Creator gives us no rehearsals for the script He writes for our lives. He is the true Author and Finisher of all, and He writes the best stories. His plans for us are brilliant. The blueprints for our life stories are diligently created by Him, and He has thought up every last detail. All the pages of our bios have been sequentially numbered before we were even born—before this day ever came to pass. In His time, our God will make Himself known to each of us in a special way.

My desire is to be a light in a dark world. "Let your light so shine before men, that they may see your good works, and glorify your Father in heaven. This is the condemnation, that light has come into the world, and men loved darkness rather than light, because their deeds were evil" (John 3:19). I will always choose truth, light, and life over lies, darkness, and death.

One of my favorite phrases in the Bible is Psalm 37:4: "Delight thyself also in the Lord; and He shall give thee the desires of thine heart." As I delighted myself in the Lord, He granted me my heart's desire. My authority comes from the Lord. I believe I have been given His authority to share this message.

God saw that something was left unfinished. I had some unresolved issues regarding matters of the heart. Like Paul in the Bible, these issues became a thorn in the flesh. God offered me an opportunity in my Kairos moment, a supreme moment divinely designed by God to fulfill my purpose and complete the work He had ordained for me. This was His assignment for me. Whenever God gives us a thing to do, He always gives us the grace to do it. I feel that the appointed time has come, and I am now ready to do this. God has gifted me to do it. Psalm 37:5 says, "Commit thy way unto the Lord; trust also in Him; and He shall bring it to pass."

An opportunity presented itself, and by the prompting of God's Holy Spirit, I seized the God-given opportunity at the most perfect time. God provided me with His divine assistance, and I began to flow under the power of His anointing. This anointing caused me to begin and complete the good work the Lord began in me. I am confident that "He who hath begun a good work in you will perform it until the day of Jesus Christ" (Phil. 1:6). My help comes from the Lord. There is no doubt in my mind that this is the appointed time God has set for me to fulfill my purpose to glorify Him. In this time—the *Fullness of Time*—I received my deliverance.

"In the beginning was the Word and the Word was with God, and the Word was God" (Gen. 1:1). "In the beginning God created the heaven and the earth" (Col. 1:16). "For by Him were all things created, that are in heaven and in earth, visible and invisible, whether they be thrones, or dominions, or principalities, or powers: All things were created by Him and for Him. So, God created all things; He created us" (Gen. 1:27).

God created man in His own image. He created males and females, our parents, the just and the unjust, and the good and the bad. He created me, my loving husband (Decell), my ex-boyfriend (Oldie), Oldie's wife and my rival for more than forty years (Sindi), Sindi's cousin (Angryd), and Decell's ex-girlfriend and my part-time rival. We all have similar cultural backgrounds since we were all born on a beautiful Caribbean island.

My name is Princess Delight. I am the wife of Decell, the ex-girlfriend and long-lost love (LLL) of Oldie, the rival of Sindi (Oldie's wife), the rival of Angryd, and Decell's ex-girlfriend and LLL. I am here to share with you my testimony about the goodness of the Lord in my life—in the land of the living.

I am also sharing my truth with you about my relationship with God. He is my Abba/Father, El Elyon, the Most High God, the Great I AM, El Roi, and the God who sees All and Knows All. He knows what goes on with all of us in our hearts and minds. He even knows our innermost secret thoughts.

Fullness of Time is a unique book because it reveals certain attributes of God in a one stop easy read. These attributes of God's grace, love, omnipotence, omniscience, mercy, presence and sovereignty are identified by the acronym 'GLOOMPS', and are found in one package, one testimony, one story, and one delivery (PTSD). The book is about five ordinary people. None of us are famous, perfect or sinless—but some of us display symptoms related to a condition known as

Post-traumatic stress disorder. I am not a professional writer, but the Holy Spirit empowered me to write and share my testimony, which is a description of my reality as it happened.

Chapter 1

Testimony/Transparency/Truth

Sindi did her best. It turned into a major mess and my biggest test. The mess became a message, and the test became my testimony. A testimony by one definition is a profession of faith in Jesus Christ and a good witness of the Lord. It consists of character, conduct, and conversation. A testimony represents who we are on the inside.

"The heart is deceitful above all things and desperately wicked" (Jer. 17:9). We can never trick God into thinking our character is righteous when it is not. We cannot fake morality with people for very long because the authentic self will show up sooner or later, and it will display behavior and speech contrary to a child of God.

The big setup seemed to have been ordained by God. In the midst of it all, God showed up and revealed His power, presence, and goodness to me. The devil also showed up and revealed his intention to deceive, destroy, and divide. The Lord searches the face of the earth; the devil prowls around like a roaring lion seeking to devour. The Lord comes to give us life, and He gives it to us abundantly.

"The thief cometh not, but for to steal, kill and destroy, I am come that they might have life, and that they might have it more abundantly" (John 10:10).

I never quite understood the meaning of a satanic attack or spiritual warfare until I read the definition provided by one of my favorite pastors. Pastor Charles Stanley stated, "A satanic attack is a deliberate attack or assault upon an individual that is designed to cause spiritual, physical, material, or emotional harm." The goals are to destroy the Lord's purpose in believers' lives, rob us of joy and peace, and deny God in the first place. Satan is real and deceptive in his works—My God is real, alive, and active. He lives within me.

In March 2014, a life-shifting event took place. I did not plan any of it, but as the events unfolded, my quiet life was transformed. I believe this was a deliberate attack on my life by the devil. At first, I did not recognize that the trap was one of Satan's evil schemes. It came in a natural and simple way. I was totally unaware of any evil intentions and fell right into the devil's trap. For a period of time, I felt robbed of my joy and my peace. The devil and his emissary set out to completely destroy me, but the good Lord intervened and turned it around for good. "For they intended evil against thee: they imagined a mischievous device, which they are not able to perform" (Ps. 21:11). It is so amazing to observe the almightiness of God in the ordinariness of life.

It was a beautiful spring day. I reported to work as I had for the past twenty-five years. I sat at my desk and started my daily work routine. At one point, I took a short break to read my e-mail. To my shock and utter surprise,

I stumbled upon an e-mail from my first love. Oldie sent an invitation to connect with him on LinkedIn. I studied the e-mail for a while.

When I got home that evening, I mentioned it to my husband. I anxiously asked him what he thought I should do.

He said, "Ask the Holy Spirit."

I asked the Holy Spirit, and the reply was a resounding yes.

The next day, I accepted Oldie's invitation. We communicated openly for approximately three weeks. He offered me a phone number and asked me to call him.

I told him that I would call only after I sent him a lengthy note with all of my unspoken words.

Oldie agreed.

I poured out my heart and soul to him. In my writing, my heart became an open book. Unafraid and unashamed, I typed my unspoken words, said a silent prayer, and sent my lengthy note into cyberspace. Shortly after that, all hell broke loose. My quiet life was turning into a living nightmare. The devil was on a rampage.

> To: Oldie, MLLL, my trusted friend and brother in Christ:
> From: Delight

> I hope your time off from the office was restful and relaxing. I plan to take a couple of days off myself. I will be back to work on Thursday.

I could have held on to this note a bit longer before sending it, but over the weekend, I received confirmation in multiple ways to let it go! In my mind, the *Fullness of time* has come. I must release this now or never. Please understand this is all my truth. If it brings about any negatives, I pray they will be turned into positives and strengthen all involved for a greater good.

"Pray for me, as I will be praying for you. May the Joy of the Lord be your strength, may you be filled with love and the peace that passes all understanding. Above all things, May you prosper and be in good health, even as your soul prospers" (John 3:1–2).

In my heart, you'll remain my FF (friend forever). From my hands to your hands—and from my eyes to your eyes—here come my unspoken words.

Remember the song "Reunited"? Well, this one can be called "Reconnected." I thank God for allowing us the chance to reconnect. May this bring us physical, spiritual, and emotional healing in Jesus's name. Amen. The Lord will perfect that which concerns me. He allows everything to unfold at just the right time. He is faithful.

During the short time we've reconnected, I may be dumping out a whole lot of stuff on you. This is only because I feel this is the last chance I will get to say what I've always wanted to say to you—but never had the chance.

Depending on your state of mind, my unspoken words may not even matter to you anymore. They may evoke past memories and resurrect buried emotions. Good or bad? I cannot say. I have no idea where this is all leading—I don't know why things are unfolding like this, but I'm moving forward with it anyway. You are not obligated to read or respond, although I would like you to. If you choose to, please do so at your leisure. Right now, I feel as if I am on some kind of time line (not lifeline), and if I don't release what has been silently held within over more than forty years—I may run out of time and be left undone and frustrated.

The years 1977–1979 and 1998–2001 were extremely difficult for me. I did a lot of reflecting and searching. Having experienced what it was like to be thrown from a state of drunken love to sobering distress, I feel I deserve the chance to vent to you. I reached a point where I desperately wanted closure. No matter how hard I tried to obtain it (in my own way and strength), it wasn't happening. Every attempt proved futile. Eventually, I prayed. "Have thy own way, Lord." I surrendered to Him. The song "Redeemed" by Carlene Davis helped me a lot during this period. It created a soul-purging, spirit-cleansing experience that brought me tears, joy, peace, and freedom.

God has taken you, my husband, and the broken pieces of my heart and mended it all together again. Had I not experienced the hurt, pain, and trials, I would not have had a God-encountered moment and a testimony to share with my husband, my children, and you about the goodness of the Lord in the land of the living. He truly heals the brokenhearted. If we ask anything and believe, He will answer, provide, and open doors for us beyond our expectations.

I felt like a wounded warrior for a long, long time. All I ever yearned for was closure. I believe my desire for that is close to being fulfilled. Some unfinished business—relative to matters of the heart—is also about to be settled in His perfect timing. Thank you, my friend, for allowing me to deliver my heartfelt message to you. My heart will now be at peace, and I sense that all is going to be well with my soul. If the good Lord chooses to take me away from this life's journey into another soon, I'll be more ready than I was before. Thank you! Most importantly, I thank God! No one does it quite like Him, and there is none like Him. Bless His holy name!

If you ever feel the need to vent or unleash as I have done, please feel free to do so. You have that right. And what better time is there than now? We're both still here. It's a new day, a new season. Spring has sprung! Reconnected after more than forty years, and it feels like magic is in the air!

Below are my shared notes and quotes. Parts of it have been updated because some parts are no longer relevant. I always wanted to tell you these things, but I never had the opportunity.

To: MLLL—My Unspoken Words
A Moment in Time
Part I
(Rewind/Fast-Forward)

More than four decades ago, we met at a party in a small village. We celebrated this meeting, and wrote a masterpiece to each other. Remember that? I'm sorry I didn't keep a copy as a keepsake. I met you when I was fifteen years old. You entered my life as a lover and then as a friend. You were the most gorgeous guy I had ever met. In my eyes, you were perfect and could do no wrong. I used you as a measuring stick when it came to dating other guys. That was sort of unfair to them because there was no one else like you.

Over thirty years ago, I met my husband through you. You entered my life again. This time, you were a friend and matchmaker who was looking out for my best interests. Had it not been for God and you, my husband and I would never have met. Is that divine intervention or what? I think it is!

I love my husband. He entered my life first as a friend and then as a lover. The similarities I've experienced with the two of you are amazing! What is it about the two of you that is so intriguing? The more I think about it, the more I see this to be the work of the Almighty. This world is just not big enough for all of us.

In order to remain morally grounded, God placed someone just as unique as you in my life. This made all the difference and has everything to do with the way things are. Had it not been for him, staying in touch with you would have been impossible.

As it is now, you and I are neither lovers nor strangers. What are we to each other? There are times when my heart and soul are at unrest, wandering around and searching for the final chapter of our relationship. It faded, but it never really ended. When will it end? Where does it end? They say that true love doesn't have a happy ending. They say true love has no end. I really don't know! Do you? They also say true happiness is not having what you want. It is wanting what you have. I have experienced this to be true.

Please inform your children that they should never leave things hanging, especially in relationships. Advise them to always tie up any loose ends. They'll enjoy fuller and richer lives—and never have to wonder about all the what-ifs. Fondest memories!

To: MLLL—Relationship Review
A Purpose to Everything
Part II

After facing the reality of what happened, I thought I would never love again. I thought I would never experience true happiness with anyone else. I was left with a feeling of emptiness and bewilderment. There was an opening that needed closure. I had no say in the decision you made except to sink myself into wounded silence. I'll always wonder what kind of husband you turned out to be and what kind of father you are to your children. Had our relationship lasted, what would the future have been? We'll never know.

To me, our relationship mimicked the birth and death of a child. We brought it into existence. We loved and nurtured it with everything we had to muster. It was shorter than I expected (1973–1976). It was one of the best things that could have happened to me. In sheer innocence I experienced my highest high. There was no corruption, hang-ups, or guilt. I gained lifelong experiences and lasting memories.

Though I never mentioned it, I have been through all the stages of rejection. Something you may never have the chance to experience. I am no longer angry, vengeful, regretful, or mournful. To be that way would be destructive and enslaving. I have prayed about this, and I have been healed. I am thankful for the many blessings and for being able to advance to this state of realism and rebirth. Realism—because what's done is done. The past cannot be relived. Rebirth—because all the pain and hurt I endured have now been erased.

Maybe it was by the will of God that you introduced me to my husband. The union caused by you has compensated for an apparent injustice. He has brought a great sense of satisfaction and completeness to my life. His sense of humor and dedication to family are qualities I admire. His default is his love of music. His music is who he is. I know his love for music will never change. It's easier to accept this fact than to argue about it. This is similar to the love you once had for soccer.

You once mentioned that it would be nice if I had the chance to meet one of your ex-girlfriends. Kayjo and I never met, but it is ironic that your wife and I know each other. You and my husband have come to know each other as well. God is a master designer, especially in the way he has orchestrated our lives. To me, this has been a fairy tale filled with many strange twists. As the saying goes, nothing happens before its time. And sometimes things happen for the best.

There's a Part III, but I will leave that for another time. Enough has already been said for today. All names were purposely left out (to protect identities). Maybe our unspoken words can be compiled into book form and become a best seller, especially to other LLLs. You'll be the author. I'm sure it will be relatable to all who have loved and lost.

Having said all of this, I now feel a sense of relief and a bit of closure. Thank you once again for the experiences you have given me by being a part of my life. As our lives go on, you will always be remembered. Keep on doing the right thing. Keep calm, carry on, and take care!

After I launched my lengthy note, a copy landed in Sindi's hands. Unknown to Oldie and me, all our e-mail correspondences were viewed and read by others. One evening, my husband and I returned home. I remained in the car while Decell walked toward our house. As he entered the walkway, someone approached him like a big bad wolf, handed him a package, ranted some incoherent words, and scurried off into a waiting vehicle. Not one word was uttered to me. I asked my husband what it was all about.

He looked at me and said in disbelief, "That was Oldie's wife."

I was dazed, confused, and embarrassed by her entrance and exit. Sindi's appearance and disappearance occurred in a flash. It was as if some magical spell teleported her or beamed her from one place to another.

Her arrival at my house from a far country was faster than anything I had ever seen. Sindi was on a mission to seek, attack, and destroy.

After we entered our home, my husband quietly sat down and read the letter. I wanted to snatch it away from him, but I couldn't. When he was finished reading, there was a big hush in my household. It was a chilling moment that kept replaying in my mind. I never saw it coming! My oldest son was home at the time, and he asked if we were okay.

My husband said, "I knew some crap like this would happen! Who needs this at this time in life? Here we are both entering our golden years—looking forward to retirement—and here comes this big mess to deal with."

I asked my husband what he thought about the letter.

He said he didn't see anything wrong with it.

Although I felt relieved, I was frustrated and frazzled. I felt stupid on the inside. Nobody understood how I felt. The entire event was awkward, unforeseen, unnecessary, and unbelievable. I pleaded with the Lord to help me learn my lesson quickly. As a couple, we had never experienced that type of chaos. Perhaps God wanted to add some element of excitement and drama to our peaceful life. I could have used something a little less dramatic. Who am I to question the works of God? He already knew the outcome of all this, and everything was happening *in His perfect time*.

The days following Sindi's appearance were not easy. One of my sons seriously injured his foot in a freak accident and was incapacitated for several weeks.

Another one of my sons experienced a sprained ankle and had to be off his feet for quite some time.

I started receiving a bombardment of e-mails from Sindi. They were sent to my work e-mail account. Like a squatter, Sindi came in uninvited and took up residence on my work e-mail address. I was irritated by the constant flow of e-mails. It was a huge distraction and interruption for me at work. The e-mails were filled with blistering insults. Sindy accused me of everything you can imagine and some things you cannot.

As if that wasn't enough, she started to stalk me at home. She continuously called my home. My life was becoming messy and stressful. I could no longer find any peace. I was being harassed.

I turned it all over to the Lord. I allowed Him to take full control. The e-mails and phone calls continued from April until September. I went to work daily, dreading the e-mails. Sindi missed the whole point of my closure notes sent, and she made certain she got her point across. She mentioned that she would be my worst nightmare, and she was turning out to be just that! Sindi threatened to tell all and send copies of my e-mails to my close relatives. Little did she know that my husband, children, and sisters were already in on the entire life-shifting event.

This was definitely a test of faith for me. Even though I had told my husband that Oldie and I were communicating, I did not tell him about the content of my closure letter. I never anticipated that it would fall into his hands. It was something I needed to address only with Oldie.

With my limited human understanding, I didn't know all the aspects of the situation I was facing. The Holy Spirit became my helper, my advisor, and my counselor. He helped me to understand the complexity of my complicated situation. I felt like Jesus when He cried out to His Father and said, "O my Father, if it be possible—let this cup pass from me; nevertheless not as I will but as thou wilt" (Matt. 26:39).

I realized the road ahead was going to be difficult, and that thought wreaked havoc on my imagination. I continued to strive to have faith. I knew that I could trust God to bring me out of that situation victoriously! His words and promises are true. He will not fail or forsake me. Therefore, I will not fear or be dismayed.

The entire event shifted my life. The shift was an epic one for me. It was not nearly as devastating as the tsunami that shifted the earth in 2004, but it was threatening. The storm filled my tranquil life and comfort zone with chaos and discomfort. I asked the Lord, "How am I going to resolve this drama of the old and the restless? All I got was silence, and the silence was deafening.

I found myself wondering how I was ever going to get out of my situation? I felt like the comfort lid on my quiet life was blown off. I questioned myself. How can I change my situation? Will my life and my marriage ever be the same? What was so wrong about what I did?

I didn't have the answers to all the questions, but I read the Word, prayed like I never prayed before, and stayed connected to my Savior. This attack drove me straight into the everlasting arms of God, and that was where I stayed. In order to fight the spiritual battle I was about to encounter, I had to remain in the arms of God. I walked closer to Him. There was no other way!

I needed to rely on the strength of the Lord. I cast all my cares and anxieties on Him. My daily Bible verse became: "The Lord is my rock, my fortress, and my deliverer, my God, my strength, in whom I will trust; my buckler, and the horn of my salvation, and my high tower" (Ps. 18:2). God became my place of safety. I found protection in Him.

My initial reaction to Sindi's behavior was to try to have a face-to-face conversation about the matter, but I worried there might be some mental issues with her. It did not make sense to reason with her. I realized I was not dealing with a normal, sober, and sane individual. I counted more than sixty angry e-mails from Sindi. These e-mails were definitely not from a place of love for my family or me. They came in the form of threats and bullying schemes.

Her offensive and hateful comments led me to believe that Sindi was locked in a state of misery, anger, and jealousy. The verbal attacks and careless words were loaded with hatred and rage. Hurt people hurt people. Sindi was acting like a predator, desperately hungry for prey—and I was the scapegoat.

"A good man out of the treasure of the heart bringeth forth good things: and an evil man out of the evil treasure bringeth forth evil things" (Matt. 12:35). In order to remain calm and free from anxiety, I had to ramp up my prayer life. It had never occurred to me that I was hated so much by a hater. My closure note opened up a deep-seated wound in Sindi. The wound needed immense healing. God alone could administer that healing. Sindi needed prayers.

I would have called it quits, turned around, and walked back into my quiet lifestyle, but there was no turning back. I had to continue with the work the Lord started in me. "Being confident of this very thing, that He which begun a good work in you will perform it until the day of Christ Jesus" (Phil. 1:6).

Sindi's big setup was turning into a huge fiasco. Slowly, she began to lose all control. The Lord stepped in and took control. All things were becoming transparent. My truth and my testimony started to unravel. When we know the truth and walk in it, we shall be set free to live in the abundant life.

I did not know what to do to stop Sindi in her sin and lawless deeds. This mean-spirited woman was stealing my joy, irritating me, and terrorizing me in every way. I came to realize it was not a job for me—it was a job for God.

When I turned it over to Him and gave Him control, I received supernatural help. It was as if heaven met earth. I began to experience an awesome sense of peace about the entire situation. I felt God's power working in me. It took me to a higher level. My faith in Him increased, and I was ushered to a deeper sense of holiness. It is true that desperate times call for desperate faith.

I would be delighted to share all of Sindi's e-mails to give you an idea of the real Sindi and her thoughts, state of mind, and character. However, the content of the language would not do justice to this book. I decided not to include any of her messages. If we meet in person, it would be my pleasure to share the notes and e-mails from Sindi. Her personality and character pulsated in her words.

As I reflected on my past, I realized that my emotions had been bottled up inside for years. I never really had the chance to express my feelings to Oldie about our relationship and how it dissolved. When I finally had the opportunity to unleash, I vented in what I called my unspoken words. All I did in my closure note was to tell my truth. All I ever wanted was closure. That was my heart's desire.

Based on how the relationship ended, I believe God saw some unfinished business. He alone knew the desires of my heart. When I delighted myself in Him, He granted me that! Closure came for me on the forty-first anniversary of the day we met. Praise God! He opened a door for me to become an impactful witness.

My testimony allowed me the opportunity to make peace with my past. I let go of my grief, and I was ushered into a new place. I felt Sindi plotted to prove her husband unfaithful, bring destruction to my marriage, divide my family, or create a big scandal. Thomas Watson wrote, "Nothing hurts the godly. All things shall cooperate for their good, and their cross shall be turned into blessings." My God is awesome!

Chapter 2

Relationship/Response/Revelation

The God I serve is not a god of confusion. He is a god of peace, and His peace can only be found in Him. He is the Prince of Peace. Satan is the prince of darkness and is on a mission to destroy, deceive, and divide. God demonstrated the power of His love to me. His love is unconditional. The devil demonstrated his love of power to me. He wants total control and when he gets it, he brings only destruction.

Oldie and Me

My first meeting with Oldie was in the spring of 1973. It was very casual. We met at a party in a small village. We built a good friendship, started dating, and fell deeply in love. I had no idea what the meeting would mean for my spiritual growth.

Back then, I could not pinpoint the reason, but in retrospect, I see that God used Oldie to help shape me into person I have become. Our relationship was for a brief season. It had to run its natural course in order for God's plan and purpose to be accomplished.

In 1975, my mom decided to join my dad in the United States. My younger sister and I had no choice. We had to leave with her. This was devastating and agonizing for me. Before I departed for the United States, a farewell party was held for me at my home. Oldie attended. We managed to enjoy the night, wondering if this was the beginning or the end of our relationship.

We danced to the song "When Will I See You Again?" The entire night was bittersweet, a mix of gratitude for good times and sorrow about the uncertainty of our future. During our relationship, Oldie and I shared and talked about everything. The time we were together may not have lasted as long as I wanted it to, but it was rewarding. We treated each other as if we were the most important people in the world. A day with each other seemed like a year, and a year felt like a day.

When I left for the United States, Oldie accompanied me to the airport. We hugged each other, fought back tears, and promised to stay in touch. In my heart, I felt that it was the last time we would be together like we used to be. We departed with a final wave and drifted out of sight.

With a lump in my throat, I boarded the plane and reminisced about our friendship and our times together. *What will the future be for us?* I sighed. *Only the Lord knows.*

After being in the United States for a year, I returned home for a short visit in 1976. Oldie and I had the time of our lives. We were inseparable. He made plans to join me in the United States, but it never materialized.

When I returned to New York, we continued to communicate. After a while, our communication ceased.

Oldie was not responding to my letters like he used to. I sensed my letters to Oldie were intercepted. It appeared that they were nabbed, read, and destroyed before they ever reached Oldie's hands.

Sindi was aware that Oldie and I were dating. She cunningly came around, bewitching and enticing him. He did not have a strong defense. Days, weeks, and months went by, and our relationship started to dwindle. Unable to comprehend it all, I crawled into a corner and wept. There were no official good-byes or spoken words—just wounded silence.

Totally depressed and heartbroken, I cried for months. What else could I have done? Time and distance were against me. Crafty Sindy had a plan, and I was alone. It was the saddest and most difficult time for me. My enthusiasm for life was gone. When love is lost, we tend to love life less. I spiraled down into my wilderness. In the wilderness, I mourned the loss of my good friend. He was unique and understanding. Our relationship was not based on each other's achievements or status. We accepted each other just as we were, being true to ourselves.

I felt betrayed by Oldie's actions, but as time went by, I was able to forgive my betrayer. After many years, I realized I could not stay in my wilderness. I reluctantly moved on.

"Lord, grant me the serenity to accept the things I cannot change, courage to change the things that I can, and the wisdom to know the difference." That prayer helped me tremendously when Oldie became involved with Sindi. In doing so, he inherited new responsibilities.

I had to release him into the hands of God—just as I released my new situation into God's capable hands.

I would never forget how much Oldie inspired me. In my wilderness experience, I came to understand that God truly gives us the people we need to help us, hurt us, leave us, and love us. He wants to make us into the people we were meant to be for His glory. Maybe Oldie came into my life to teach me how to love better, stronger, and wiser the second time for all the right reasons.

I believe I entered Oldie's life to teach him how to love the unlovable and demonstrate unconditional love. I am no longer weeping because it is over. I am smiling because it happened. The wilderness was necessary for me; it provided me with growth and spiritual maturity. My faith in God was tested, and it transformed me into a worthy servant of God. God was preparing me for His vision. He always has our best interests at heart.

Decell and Me

My meeting with Decell was unplanned and unexpected. We met in 1979 when Oldie came to New York. Oldie managed to make a quick escape from Sindi. He visited me at my home with his friend Decell. It was my first time seeing Oldie since 1976. It was a strange experience! He was officially a married man.

When I met Decell, I was twenty-two years old, depressed, and hurt. The thought of being involved in another romantic relationship was the furthest thing from my mind. I was a broken vessel with broken mind, body, and spirit, and my heart was becoming hardened. I felt that I had nothing to offer anyone.

After our first meeting, whenever Decell visited my neighborhood, he would stop by to see me. As time went by, I started looking forward to his visits. I really began to enjoy his company. We went out on a couple dates. Decell made me laugh a lot. His sense of humor was refreshing, and it still is! He made me realize that laughter is medicine for the soul.

With the help of God and Decell's humor, my broken spirit was lifted. Bit by bit, Decell assisted in rebuilding my heart, allowing me to trust and love again. He caused me to review the trauma of my previous relationship without any negativity. He listened to my sad story about my past and was not impressed or intimidated by it. Instead, he embraced and accepted me just as I was. His compassion brought healing, which assured me that this too shall pass. Indeed, it did!

I felt new again. God was working all things out for our good. In all things—the good, the bad, and the ugly—I give God thanks and praise.

As time went by, Decell and I grew closer. We became good friends. Slowly, I began falling in love with him. He is now my loving and supportive husband, a great father to our four children, and a wonderful grandfather to our five grandchildren. If he had walked away and left me to myself in my brokenness, I would have missed out on so much. We are a blessed family.

God has used my past for His purpose. He is God, and He is good. I will forever praise Him. In order to enter a new place, I had to let go of my grief and pain and trust in the Lord's leading.

Decell and I have been together for more than thirty-five years. He calls me his queen, and when he does, it makes me think of my mom, Aunt V, my mother-in-law, and one of my sisters. These women have been my role models. They are royal and are truly worthy of queenly status. "A virtuous woman is a crown to her husband; but she that maketh ashamed is as rottenness in his bones" (Prov. 12:4).

Decell and I love and respect each other. We are committed to each other, and we will continue to work to make our marriage stronger and make it last—no matter what! My prayer daily for us is that the Lord will teach us how to love like He loves and give us pure hearts with good motives.

Oldie and Sindi

When I left my little island in 1976, Sindi befriended Oldie. He was a great catch. Her plots and plans worked. Sindi became pregnant, and Oldie did the right thing. He married Sindi and made her his wife. I imagined that they were happily married and enjoying life.

As the years went by, I was told that Sindi became a nagging wife, a fervent husband-watcher, and a malicious woman attacker. She was boastful, a great social media companion, and a bully, especially when it came to women who were friends with her husband.

After years of being married and raising five children, Sindi developed more good points. Her husband-watching/stalking activities and incessant nagging escalated. After an especially trying time, Sindi's woman-chasing/attacking/stalking showdown befell Delight and Decell. When Oldie found out about this, he was humiliated and embarrassed. I felt badly for him. He had become a scarred man, living as a hostage in the bondage of marriage and home. Oldie was an intelligent man, but he couldn't escape the chains of manipulation and deception that enslaved him.

I dreamed that Sindi was stalking someone, and her own husband almost ran her over in her driveway. In my dream, the stalking came to a halt for a short while. Sindi lived to tell the tale. I wondered if the dream was real. All my problems would have been solved! I wondered if there was any good in it. I had an a-ha moment. It dawned on me that God had a plan and a purpose. Oldie had to take Sindi as his wife because she had a purpose to fulfill. Oldie had to train her so that she could fulfill her purpose of drawing Him to the Lord.

Sindi fulfilled her purpose of drawing Oldie to God, and in some mysterious way, she also caused me to draw closer to the Lord. Whenever I think of Sindi and remember her behavior, I smile and think of Romans, 8:28: "All things work for good to them that love God, to them who are the called according to His purpose."

"Every wise woman buildeth her house: but the foolish plucketh it down with her hands" (Prov. 14:1). Sindi's behavior brought on her demise. She transformed from being Oldie's wife and queen to an evil queen. She slid down the slippery slope into a fool's paradise where she became a fool for a lifetime.

When God wants to accomplish something or has a mission, He looks for someone to take the assignment. Perhaps God's job for Sindi was to accomplish the task of drawing us all closer to Him. Who knows? Maybe we have all come to the kingdom for such a time as this, and because of this, God has caused my husband and my sons to witness the power of God and show them evidence of His presence in our lives. Perhaps God wanted to show us all who He was, how He works, and to what extremes He would go to bring us all back to Him. Nothing can duplicate the evidence of God's power and His presence. May God continue to equip us for whatever He has called us to do.

Decell and Angryd

I don't know when Decell and Angryd met or how long their relationship lasted. I do not know very much about Angryd except that she is a cousin of Sindi. When I met Decell in 1979, he and Angryd were on the verge of ending their relationship.

While Decell and I were building our friendship, Angryd became pregnant with another man's child. She went around boasting that she and Decell would get back together once she had the baby. As much as she wanted that to be, it never happened. When Angryd acknowledged that Decell and I were dating, she harassed me over the phone on a daily basis for months. The harassment only stopped when Decell said enough was enough and changed his number.

With the new number, the harassment stopped. For years, Angryd tried to destroy my relationship with Decell. It was in her best interests to distract us and keep us divided, but my God intervened and dismantled her plans. The Word of God says we are to bless those who persecute us—and bless and do not curse them (Rom. 12:14).

For whatever reason, I am Sindi and Angryd's primary target. They seem obsessed with attacking me. Though not intentional, my closure letter provoked an attack. Sindi and Angryd made a concerted attempt to intimidate me, defame me, and smear my name. They thought I was a patsy. Today, Angryd has children. I do not know if she's married. She may still be living in the past since she posted pictures of herself with Decell (from when they were dating) on Facebook. Who knows? She may be bitter and angry like Sindi and living in a state of hostility. Angryd may also be in need of deliverance from the ghosts of yesteryears.

I believe that God has called us all for this moment in time. In this supreme moment, everything is happening according to His plan. If we walk with Him, He will reveal His plans and His purpose to us. His plans are for us to prosper and not be harmed. I am ready. I will walk boldly for He is my Jehovah Rohi.

The Lord leads and guides me. He has brought me here for a greater purpose. He has been with me from the very beginning of my life, and He will be with me until the end of my journey. When I am lost, He is the shepherd who goes looking for the lost sheep.

The devil's reign is over. Christ is on the throne. This is the day the Lord has made, and I will rejoice and be glad in it. A day is coming when the wicked will expect great joy, but there will be cries of anguish and great sadness because of their sins and rebellious ways. God has delivered me, and I know He can deliver sinners and the demonized. He works in our lives according to our faith. Use me, Lord, as an instrument to bring deliverance to those who are enslaved and lost. The stone that the builders reject has become the chief cornerstone.

I am thankful that my God found me when He did. In His awesomeness, He brought families together to reveal Himself to all in an extraordinary way. How great is God? He unites all things in heaven and on earth to Him—in the *Fullness of Time, in His Perfect Time.*

For months, the e-mails from Sindi caused physical, emotional, and mental stress. I wanted all the chaos to end, but the end was nowhere in sight. Many days, I prayed and said, "Father God, only you can help me—only you can bring this all to an end. I surrender all I am and all I have to you. Please take full control of this. This battle is yours, Lord, not mine."

I placed the entire situation in His hands and left it there. My flesh wanted to respond so badly to some of Sindi's e-mails, but the Lord kept me grounded. The Holy Spirit gave me wise counsel. He told me to wait on the Lord. I waited for more than six months!

After the long wait, I was prompted to write a letter to Sindi's husband. I wrote the letter and hoped Sindi would change her behavior and have a total heart transformation. She was falling deeper and deeper into sin and lawlessness. The Lord revealed so much to me. Instead of living dynamically, Sindi was imitating a dynamic lifestyle. She was living a life of pretense. I read that love given reflects love received. Sindi could not receive the love she was given or show genuine affection. She appeared lonely and angry. She was looking to blame someone else for her unhappiness. Regardless of the real contributors to her mental and marital woes, I was the primary target.

Unknown to Oldie, Sindi was sending me hourly e-mails on a daily basis. After receiving a collection of bullying e-mails from Sindi, the Holy Spirit encouraged me to write a letter to Oldie.

To: Oldie
From: Delight

Hey—good day to you! Hope all's going well. This is the fastest reunited/reconnected/disconnected session I have witnessed in years.

Just to let you know, your wife Sindi has been sending me e-mails from April through September 2014. There's no reason to read or respond to any of these (the contents are offensive to God and man). If needed, all can be forwarded to you—so you can understand the situation with a bit more clarity.

Soon I will be approaching my golden years, and my heart's desire is to start cleaning up my heart and my act on earth in preparation to meet my Maker in the place He has prepared for me.

I have no desire to compete, compare, or prove anything. I am a child of God, a daughter of the King. Just knowing that is enough for me. It puts me in a place where I am at peace. God sees us as plain as we are—and nothing is ever hidden from Him. I hope our conscience also sees us as plain as we are.

I once saw a sign by a church: "No God—no peace, no love, no truth. Only in knowing Him can we truly know His peace, His love, and His truth." I pray that all of us will come to experience God's love and His blessings in a new way.

When a person wants to truly advertise his or her ignorance, there is nothing we need to do or say except wait. If you let the person talk, write, and expose the self, the truth of self will be revealed.

I was wondering how long it would take for the true person to stand up and show off. In the e-mails, the true person showed up in a grand way, revealed the authentic self, and showed the makeup of her heart and character.

As a man thinks in his heart, so is he! Based on the contents of the e-mails, it appears that the sender is playing her own god and acting like the lord of the earth without the Lord in heaven. She is manipulating and controlling people with her words.

In the eyes of God, all our advantages and righteousness are nothing but filthy rags. It is only when we surrender all to Him that He moves in to help us—and we begin to see how real He is. He clothes us in His righteousness and makes us new. He does the work in us and for us! It's like an extreme makeover.

I really couldn't fix myself, but when Jesus found me, He took hold of me and did the work from inside out. I knew I had been changed, and it was only by His grace! There comes a time when a person should realize that his or her attempts did not bring about the expected results or satisfaction.

Maybe it's time to give Jesus a try (wholeheartedly). He is the final link, and He fixes us better than we could imagine. He did it for me, and He continues doing it! I am still a work in progress. What He has done for me, He can surely do for others! I pray the Lord continues to deliver us all from bondage. We all will come to know the one true and living

God whose grace is sufficient for every situation.

In all things, give thanks!

Before ending, I will share some quotes with you.

- When there is love and God's righteousness in the heart, there will be beauty in the character.
- The best way to find out if we can trust someone is to simply trust him or her.
- Be true to yourself.
- Don't forget to laugh, live, love, forgive, and help someone when you can.
- Friends are like stars—even though we don't see them, we know they are always there.

Grace and peace!

Three days after I mailed the letter to her husband's work address, the e-mails stopped. Although it was only for a while, I celebrated and praised God. He is a present help in times of trouble, and He is great!

Sindi came into my life unannounced, uninvited, and unexpected. She was like a madwoman with a pack of nonsense. She acted like an unrepentant troublemaker who was out to harass me and hurt others. She was now in a no-win situation. I almost began to feel sorry for her.

She needed a change of mind, attitude, and heart. Only God could bring about those types of changes.

She made a grand entrance into my life with her e-mails and other schemes, but none of it worked as she expected. She ended up tumbling violently into the ditch she dug for me. I thank God for being who He is. He meets us in our mess and turns it into a message.

God allowed me to cross paths with Sindi for the purpose of leading others to Him. It was all for His glory. I could not have done it on my own—even if I tried.

Chapter 3

Ultimate Silence/Unspoken Words/Until Now

Sindi haunted and hunted me for more than six months. She tormented and harassed me with e-mails. She stalked and preyed on me while I talked and prayed. I asked God to bring an end to the fiasco. I waited for her to stop the e-mails, but that was never going to happen. I concluded that Sindi was probably very surprised, annoyed, or amused at my lack of replies to her bullying e-mails. They were filled with hatred. I began to wonder why she had become disgruntled and dysfunctional over the years. I cannot say for certain, but her grudge was obvious. Something messed up Sindi's mind, and she became vengeful, sad, and lonely. She really needed attention! Her life and marriage were depraved, and she was set on causing a deep shift in my life and my marriage. That woman was ticked off at someone for years—and that someone turned out to be me.

I couldn't call my friends for help. My situation was beyond that. I needed to go to God. I communed with God, and I found peace. I remained silent in His presence.

He whispered, "Be still and know that I am God."

I remained calm and listened to His whispers. In silence, God revealed Himself to me. I had to rely on Him completely. I became still, and I placed myself before the King of Kings. I prayed and asked Him to act on my behalf. I learned something new about God and how He operates. "And thine ears shall hear a word behind thee, saying, 'This is the way, walk ye in it, when ye turn to the right hand and when ye turn to the left'" (Isa. 30:21).

No matter how the Lord directs me, I will choose to follow Him. I will trust Him and do exactly as He says. He will never mislead me. He is the one I can depend on every time and in every situation. In silence, I prayed for guidance, strength, knowledge, and wisdom. God provided me with all that I asked. He instructed me to be bold as a lion, wise as a serpent, and gentle as a dove. I prayed for the Holy Spirit to indwell me. Whenever I am indwelt with the Holy Spirit, I know who I belong to. I know I am secure and authentic because He is real.

With a husband, four children, five grandchildren, and a dog, my daily life is filled with noise. When I retreat from the noise and the busyness of life, I enter a quiet place of rest. I can hear God's voice speaking clearly to me through His Spirit. When this happens, I cannot ignore the voice of my Creator. It is real, and it has purpose. It has been said that God's voice can be heard in the scriptures, songs, melodies, nature, and silence. I believe it with all my heart.

Silence is sometimes a profound and appropriate act. Martin Luther King said, "In the end, it is not the hurtful words of our enemies we will remember, but the silence of our friends."

I believe the stage was set for all of this before I even began to experience it. Ultimate silence has been evident to me for quite some time. I do not question the reason for it. The time has come for me to reflect and to give thanks.

I often think of my high school English teacher. Ms. Bernadette was a great teacher who believed in her students and always pushed us to do our very best. May God bless her. In my heart, I always wanted to write, but I was never able to accomplish it on my own until now. My unspoken words have been spoken. The chapters of my book have been written, and my book is done. My first assignment from God has been completed, and I thank God for choosing me to fulfill this purpose. Pastor A. R Bernard said, "Whatever God has gifted you to do, He has purposed you to do."

Intimacy with God gives us a divine view of things with divine peace. I will quiet my mind and listen to what God has to say. Before God gives us an assignment, He will examine the object of our desire and place it in our hands. God has taken my past and turned it into purpose. "Let the redeemed of the Lord say so—whom He hath redeemed from the hand of the enemy" (Ps. 107:2).

During the spring of 2014, in my quiet time one weekend, a compelling voice told me to go share.

Share what and with whom? Certainly not me, Lord, and definitely not to them. I remained silent, and I began to receive confirmation in multiple ways from God that I should go on and share my testimony. I really did not want to do it because I did not want to be vulnerable.

I did not want to be transparent, but I could not ignore the voice. I really preferred to keep it a secret, but the urge was too strong to resist. I am sharing what the Holy Spirit prompted me to do. I think I did what the Lord commanded me to do in the right manner and in the right time—my appointed time. It was my Kairos moment.

With the help of Decell, Oldie, Sindi, and Angryd, I accepted God's call to fulfill this purpose. My obedience to God's calling is now my testimony to my husband, my children, my sisters, my brothers, and my loved ones. God can really take what the devil meant for evil and use it all for our good and for His glory. God knows all truth at all times. He will make all things right—all in His time. In the *Fullness of Time*, He makes all things beautiful. Praise His holy name!

Father God, I am in awe of Your transforming power in my life. I feel as if I have fulfilled one of Your God-given missions to go and share my story. I became transparent before You and others. You showed up and displayed Your goodness and Your love when I needed it most. I will forever thank and praise You. I have been blessed with Your peace, joy, and contentment. I will magnify You, Lord, forever!

Chapter 4

Calamity/Christ's Calling/Complete Closure

Sindi's goals were to destroy my family and me and make my life miserable. God's divine intention was to reveal Himself to Sindi, others, and me. I thank Almighty God for His wondrous work in my life and in the lives of others.

Throughout my years, I have experienced three huge distractions that grab my attention in the worst way. Mosquitos, bats, and Chihuahuas bring extreme frustration and annoyance to me. The mosquito will come upon me when I begin to find perfect rest on a hot summer day or night. It will annoy me with constant buzzing in my ear and will not stop until I swat it or allow it to escape through an open window, saving it from death. The bat wreaked havoc at a barbecue by constantly flying over my head and disturbing my peace. The disturbance became so painfully offensive that I ended up leaving the barbecue, wishing that somebody had the nerve to kill the darn bat. Upon further examination, I realized that bats have a purpose. I felt a tinge of sorrow for the creature. I asked God for His forgiveness for my thoughts.

A little Chihuahua passes my home every day. He barks incessantly at my German shepherd. Tazzo ignored him for months. One day, Tazzo had enough. As the small dog passed by and started to bark, Tazzo leaped for it. Before I knew it, the small dog's head was clasped in Tazzo's jaws.

I yelled, "No! Tazzo! Stop!" If I had not intervened, Tazzo could have bitten off the head of the Chihuahua, resulting in death. Both dogs could have died—one for provoking the other to anger and the other for failing to control his anger. My intervention and a bit of discipline offered the dogs a chance to live. I hope they both learned a valuable lesson that day.

That situation reminded me a lot of Sindi and me. In many ways, Sindi reminds me of these annoyances. Just as I intervened with the dogs, God intervenes in our lives to stop our sinful ways. Some of us will heed God's discipline, but others will continue in sin and rebelliousness. Sindi is still one of my biggest distractions and attention grabbers. It must be the only attention she gets. Her goal was to slander, demean, torment, and defame me for a forty-year grudge. Sindi did not care about truth or integrity. She was like the queen of evil who was disguised as an angel. She was successful in carrying out her schemes.

"Do you see a man wise in his own eyes? There is more hope for a fool than for him" (Prov. 26:12).

"There is a way that seems right to a man, but its end is the way of death" (Prov. 14:12).

If we do the same things for forty years with the same results, maybe we should try something different.

While Sindi continued in her sin, the Lord was working in me. He was showing me His grace, and I was growing in graciousness. I wondered what it would take for Sindi to change her ways. It is never too late to start over. If we are not happy with our yesterdays, we can always try something different. Sindi is stuck in her yesterdays.

The e-mails from Sindi became tiring. I did not initiate the writing to her. I did not contact her. She was irrelevant to what transpired between Oldie and me. I felt I had to make amends with Oldie. Sindi claimed to have set up the LinkedIn account for Oldie to get in touch with me. I may never know her motives.

Sindi ended up falling into her own trap. None of us are innocent, and we all play our parts in this event. Perhaps it unfolded just the way God orchestrated it, and calamity came to all. None of us expected this soap opera/drama to play out as it did.

I knew the Holy Spirit was present throughout the entire situation, but it was still traumatic and exhausting. As a married woman with grown children, I never thought I would have to deal with cybercrime or encounter a cyber-stalker/bully. I was not Sindi's first victim, and I might not be her last. God knows all about her. She enjoyed flirting with sin. Her strength was in her words, but they were lies. She picked me as her target because she thought she would have power over me. Clearly, she did not understand the power of God. He advised me to be the more mature person and say nothing, do nothing, and move only when He prompted me to move. Maybe her marriage was under some kind of stress or needed restructuring.

Some married couples try to ignore the fact that their marriage is on the verge of collapsing and pretend everything is okay. Pretending is extremely hard work! We can fool some of the people some of the time, but not all the people all the time. God can fix anything, and if we talk to Him and offer Him our marriages, He will restore it and bless us beyond our expectations. He always does!

If Sindi's marriage is broken, she needs to work at fixing it and leave my family alone. Perhaps she could request a meeting with Ms. Iyanla Vanzant, a spiritual teacher, life coach and counselor who assists those in relationship crises. This may help improve Sindi's life and her marriage for a greater good. I am so very blessed to be married to Decell. He fills my life with love, laughter, joy, and music. Meeting him was a gift. When we met, it felt like we had already known each other for a long time. We fit together naturally. It was as if our meeting was predestined. As our lives continue to grow, I am becoming more and more aware of how blessed I am to share my life with Decell. So many people are still searching for what we have. All of me loves all of him.

Christ showed up and revealed Himself to me. I am convinced that this life-shifting event was divinely designed and mapped out with God's purpose and plan—just for me! The Lord gave me spiritual vision, wisdom, and discernment to see, and I saw the One who always sees me. My God is real, alive, and active. He is El Roi. He sees me. He sees all that I am because He is the Great I AM.

God examined my past for a better future. I am now walking in my newfound freedom because I have made peace with my past. God listens and answers prayers, and He truly satisfies the desires of our hearts. All things are working for His good, and His favor is upon me. God chooses the foolish things of the world to shame the wise. All of this was for a higher calling.

"I am crucified with Christ: nevertheless I live; yet not I but Christ liveth in me" (Gal. 2:20).

His invisible hands guide me. He is in control of me. His spirit residing in me causes me to live a God-infused, God-empowered life. I was no match for Sindi. I could not handle her on my own because I am an introvert. I am more of a behind-the-scenes person. I don't like to draw attention to myself. I don't see myself as confrontational, manipulative, or dramatic. I stepped into this event by faith, relying on God's promise that He will never leave me. God stepped into our tangled web to save us all from sin and bring us abundant life. My testimony has allowed me to let go of the grief of my past and enter a new place. I refuse to participate in the powers of darkness.

God is my life and brings light to my world. Sindi presented me with a platform to witness and tell the good news. May my testimony be an inspiration for all to search for the deep things of God. This is my eyewitness account of my relationship with my Father.

When I started to write the letter to Oldie, the Spirit of the Lord said to me, "Do not worry about what you will say or how you will say it. The right words will be there."

The Spirit of God supplied me with all the words. I knew I was representing God.

He said, "Don't be intimidated. Eventually everything will be out in the open, and everyone will know how things really are. Do not be bullied into silence by threats. Nothing can be done to your soul or your core being."

One of my sisters reminded me of "Lord, I Offer My Life to You" by Hillsong. If you ever have the chance, please listen to it. The song explains my story very well.

God holds my entire life, body, and soul in His hands. "There are many devices in a man's heart: nevertheless the counsel of the Lord, that shall stand" (Prov. 19:21).

I have experienced many losses in my life, and I have lived long enough to know that life is short. I do not have the time to indulge in fake butter, artificial sweeteners, or phony people. They are all insignificant to my purpose. My God is real, and my desire is to be like Him.

I have come to realize that Sindi is a fraud, a control freak, a hypocrite, and an imposter. With all of this, she represents the devil who is a liar and the father of lies. "Bread of deceit is sweet to a man: but afterwards his mouth shall be filled with gravel" (Prov. 20:17).

"Ye are of your father, the devil, and the lusts of your father ye will do. He was a murderer from the beginning and abode not in the truth, because there is no truth in him. When he speaketh a lie, he speaketh of his own: for he is a liar, and the father of it" (John 8:44). I pray for Sindi's deliverance.

God operates on His timetable. Whatever gifts He has given me, I must use them to edify others. We cannot hide and cherish sin and expect God to hear and answer our prayers. God saw all of it coming, and He knew the outcome.

The evil that men do lives after them—even while they are alive—and the righteous sometimes will see the goodness of the Lord in the land of the living. God knows us all. He knows the mind of every one of us. He sees the conflict for what it really is and what it appears to be. When God reveals the time for victory, we can shout for joy for His timing is always perfect.

God's plan is certain, and it never collapses. It includes all the insignificant details of the past, present, and our future. The satisfaction for me in all of this is that God clearly saw my motives and my intentions. I went into this with a clear conscience and clean hands, and I came out of it with clean hands and a pure heart.

One of my dad's famous quotes was, "Whatever you do, do it, with clean hands and a pure heart"—My father will be proud to see that I obeyed him in this. "He that hath clean hands, and a pure heart: who hat not lifted up his soul unto vanity, nor sworn deceitfully, he shall receive blessing from the Lord, and righteousness from the God of his salvation" (Ps. 24:4–5). My God is Sovereign and He controls all. He will reveal all things at the appointed time, in the *Fullness of Time—In His Perfect Time.*

"Arise, shine: for the light is come, and the glory of the Lord is risen upon thee" (Isa. 60:1).

I believe all this happened so that the work of God could be displayed in our lives. God saw this as an opportunity to do something for someone who was hurting. Sindi was oblivious of the distorted anger and hatred indwelling her, and she allowed vengeance to become a driving force. As for me, I am no longer the person I used to be. I have accepted Jesus Christ as my Savior, and He has changed me. He came to me in my blindness, weakness, and my pain. He touched me. This caused me to believe in Him and worship Him in spirit and in truth. I may not know very much, but I know what the good Lord has done for me. He has become my rock and my fortress. He freed me from the net that was secretly set for me by Satan and Sindi. God is my refuge.

Looking back, I see that God set this entire plan in motion. We all came into this world helpless and naked. We showed up, and God took full control of our lives. He knew the battles we would face. He knows our beginnings and our endings. He knows all things! God truly governs all the affairs of men.

In the spring of 1973, I met Oldie. In the spring of 2014, I sent my closure letter to him. That moment became a time of testing for me, and the test became my testimony. During that time—*Fullness of Time*—I received complete closure and entered into a dark place in Sindi's world. It was the time to demonstrate the light of God to her. I believe Sindi's sin was about to find her. Nothing she did surprised God, and nothing escaped His eyes. The reunion was a meeting of minds, spirits, personalities, and families. When Sindi received knowledge of my letter, I hope the binding shackles and chains of sin and slavery were broken and deliverance and salvation came to all, including Sindi and her family.

God works in mysterious ways, and He causes all things to work together for our good—the hard things, the embarrassing things, the overwhelming things, and the very bad things. All things work together for our good. I rode out 2014 by thinking that the end had come to this cheap drama. I was beginning to feel refreshed. I looked forward to new and better things in 2015.

In January 2015, I received a request for my personal e-mail address from Oldie. I thought Oldie might have had some unspoken words to voice. Uncertain, I offered my personal e-mail address. I communicated with the holder of the e-mail address for approximately two weeks. All along, I thought I was communicating with Oldie.

Suddenly, the Holy Spirit quickened me. I was awakened to the fact that I had not been communicating with Oldie. It was Sindi! I could not believe deceitful Sindi had duped me again. Satan and Sindi's reign were drawing near, and the deception intensified. Sindi was impersonating her own husband, and I fell into her scheme.

The Holy Spirit was guiding me all along, and I didn't say anything I regretted. In my responses, I spoke from my heart. This time, my crime was in my ignorance. I thought I was chatting with Oldie, but it was Sindi. I felt extremely stupid, but I did not worry too long. I was convinced that God had it! I paused and laughed and prayed. "All yours, Lord. Lead me through this one—as only you can—and I will follow."

Sindi was dabbling in sin. She was caught up in it—much deeper that she even knew. Satan was an imposter—and Sindi was too. God knew it, and He was no longer willing to tolerate it. Did Oldie know it? I do not know. The one thing I do know is that the Holy Spirit was ready to bring Sindi's sinfulness and wrong behavior to her attention. Sindi's sin would now be dealt with.

Jesus was ready to do the work in her. He would remove the layers and strip away all that needed to be removed until all was laid bare before God. For Sindi, it would be a time of cleansing and purging. It would be a kind of open-heart surgery. There would be no more pretending, hiding, or covering up. It would be a time of total exposure. Authenticity and truth would be revealed. A day of revelation had come. Sindi would have the chance to trade her weakness and her wickedness for God's compassion, mercy, and grace. The true test of self and who we are is revealed in what we do when we are absolutely certain we will not be caught.

In January 2015, I mailed another note to Oldie.

> To: Oldie
> From: Delight
>
> Good day, Mr. Oldie:
> A blessed day to you. I do hope 2015 started off as a year of refreshment to you and yours. This is another visit from the phantom writer. Please see e-mail conversations that transpired in January 2015. Originally, I thought these e-mails were from you, but after careful review, I am led to believe that you are being impersonated.

I hope you will take the time to read the entire conversation and decide what can be done to put an end to all the madness. My crime always ends up being my ignorance. Whether this is really you or not, the attempt to nullify or negate the existence of this relationship is foolish. It has already positively impacted my life, and I am a better—not bitter—person because of it.

Albert Einstein said, "Only two things are infinite, the universe and human stupidity, and I'm not sure about the first, but of the second, I am now certain!"

My husband says, "It makes one wonder to what length a person would go to prove his or her own stupidity and lawless deeds."

I do not wish to bring you any more humiliation or embarrassment, but Mrs. Big Stuff either does not value her freedom or her life with her family. Human nature always wants to be in control, but God is God—and we are not. Mrs. Big Stuff seems to think she is above God and the law. Perhaps when both catch up to her, she will have learned a great lesson and will finally become the person God created her to be.

If you ever need to contact me, please check with Mrs. Big Stuff. She has the following:

- my home address (which she has stalked many times)
- my home telephone number (which she has called numerous times)
- my work e-mail address (where she came in as a squatter and took up residence for six months)
- my private e-mail address (where she has e-mailed all of the attached).

Daily quote for the day: "The more we walk in our divine identity and in His divine ways, the more we will enjoy God's blessings and shine the Light of Jesus to lost people in a lost world."

Grace and peace!

I know for certain now that hell has no fury as a woman scorned—and earth has no pain or sorrow that heaven cannot heal. I cannot say for sure that Oldie read the note or if he will ever provide a response, but I know that God is working out all things. I know that God has this! My husband and my sons also have this! Even the local police precinct has this.

The precious blood of Jesus covered my family. They knew about this from the beginning to the end. Should any harm ever come to me for speaking my truth, they already have an idea of the number one suspect and first person of interest. They know exactly who they should go looking for. This was a major storm for me. I thank God for being my anchor in the storm. He granted me peace, stability, wisdom, knowledge, discernment, comfort, and joy. How great is God? I need more and more of Him. I will not allow anything to stand between Jesus and me. There is power in the blood of Jesus and in His name. Jesus is the sweetest name I know.

Since February 2015, I have not heard from Sindi. At times, there have been scattered phone calls from a private/unknown caller, but it does not bother me. I have received complete closure, and this has always been the desire of my heart. I have been broken, and I have shared my testimony with you on my brokenness in the hopes that you may see how God operates in our lives.

He is sovereign, supreme, omnipotent, omniscient, and omnipresent. He is Master, Lord, and Ruler of the Universe. He knows our past, present, and our future. He understands everything about us and knows exactly what is lurking around the corner of our lives. No matter what or how things may look, God is in total control.

One of my sisters always says, "No experience in life is ever wasted. Everything that occurs happens for a purpose."

When my work here is done, I look forward to a face-to-face meeting with the Lord. Perhaps when that time comes, I will finally understand everything and get answers to all my unanswered questions. Until then, I will continue trusting in the Lord. I believe in his promise.

"The Lord will accomplish that which concerneth me: thy mercy, O Lord, endureth forever" (Ps. 138:8). My God is always working things out for the best.

As I was browsing the Internet one day, I came across the picture below. God surely has a sense of humor. Oldie and Sindi unknowingly presented me with useful notes and e-mails for my book. I have used the loaned notes as needed, and I am ready to return the same to the original lenders in the *Fullness of Time*—just as the picture below depicts.

In my mind, *Fullness of Time* has arrived. Oldie and Sindi, I render to you both the things that are yours in this full and perfect time. I want to thank you for motivating me to write this book. Now that I have completed it, I may be public enemy number one to Sindy and others, but it's all okay. I render to God all the things that are His. We are all His children. May He have His perfect way—and may His will be done in our lives. "We are his workmanship created in Christ Jesus unto good works, which God hath before ordained that we should walk in them" (Eph. 2:10).

Chapter 5

Exposure/End-All/Eternity

After I sent my official good-bye e-mail to Oldie, all hell broke loose. What the devil intended for evil, God turned it around for my good. I am so blessed. God is my solid rock, and my husband is second to Him. Because of Decell, I have become a better wife, mother, and grandmother. I am a better person because of my husband, and I am thankful for that.

For months, I was amazed to see how God showed up and revealed His power in this story. He showed his powerful presence and His perfect timing in achieving his purpose, which draws us all unto Him. The hands of God are evident everywhere. Everything has been divinely arranged and beautifully timed.

God is our designer and our coordinator. He puts it all together (people, places, time, events, and actions). Satan cannot destroy God's plan—no matter how hard he tries. God created the Universe, and He is the Divine Architect. He orders every detail of our lives to accomplish His perfect will. What a great revelation it is to know that God is still on the throne and is working all things out for us, for our good, and for His purpose.

My heart is filled with gratitude for what the Lord has done for me. I have learned that we should never underestimate God's power, authority, or wisdom. He works on our behalf, and He can undo all the works of the enemy.

Sindi came to my home uninvited. Her anger and foolish behavior were like an overgrown teenager who was crazy. Was it ego or insecurity? I do not know, but from the tone of Sindi's e-mail, it appeared that she was intoxicated with anger, hatred, and jealousy. She made threats and accusations—none of which were true. Her unresolved anger, hidden secrets, and issues came alive, and she took it as an opportunity to justify her behavior. In doing so, she became her own worst enemy.

I had some unresolved issues with Oldie, and I got to voice them in my closure note. Oldie may have had some unresolved emotions that he was able to express in his e-mails. If Decell had any questions about my love for him, the answers were all revealed in my closure note. And Angryd? I hope her issues—whatever they were—have been resolved.

God's timing is just so perfect. All of this came at a time when God had spoken to my spirit, which explains my urgency to send the closure letter. I sent it exactly forty-one years after I met Oldie. Who would know this but God? I questioned myself and knew I needed to believe in the Holy Spirit's prompting me to move. I moved as He commanded me and left all the rest in God's hands to have His perfect way. My next step didn't matter because I knew I was operating under His authority.

I was being obedient to His voice by acting on the truth given to me. I knew it was from God because I felt so much peace after e-mailing the letter to Oldie. It was the peace that one can only find in the Prince of Peace. Those seeking knowledge from the dark side from the Prince of Darkness will end up in total failure and destruction. The situation appeared to be spiritual warfare at its highest.

In no way did I indicate any involvement with that woman's husband in my letter. She was so negative in her thinking that she did not have the ability to process the information in my e-mail. Sindi was focused so much on hating me that she did not take the time to examine the context of it. She missed the deeper message. If she had listened to "Someone Like You" by Adele, she would have understood my point clearly.

I am convinced that everything that goes on in the natural happens in the supernatural—and only God can bring it all out in the open. I cannot say what God's plans are for these relationships, but I pray it will all be for greater and better things since it reveals hard truths. I am certain that all things will be made right in the *Fullness of Time—In His Perfect Time*—He will make all things bright and beautiful!

Life is to be lived authentically and with transparency. If we do not live our lives being true to ourselves, our relationships with self and others will be miserable, grumpy, depressed, and lonely. It is foolish to pretend that everything is wonderful when it is not. A life of hypocrisy is unhealthy and can lead one to a deeply troubled and complicated state.

Horace Mann said, "It is well to think well. It is divine to act well."

Socrates said, "The greatest way to live with honor in this world is to be what we pretend to be."

A sinner will continue in sin and darkness until the light of Jesus begins to shine. When it does, all the sins of the sinner will be revealed and exposed.

My brother says, "Man proposes, but God disposes and exposes all. Nothing can ever be hidden from God."

Is there going to be a sequel to this book? Maybe— if Oldie and Sindi provide me with additional notes following the redemptive encounter with Jesus. He is the one who offers salvation to all. It is our choice to continue to hold onto things we cannot keep and reject the things we cannot lose.

To live in darkness is to be living in a state where evil is. When we call on God, He will frustrate our enemies' plans and provide His people with discernment, ways of escape, and ways to avoid enemy traps.

My closure letter uprooted a lot of buried stuff for Oldie, Sindi, and me. It perhaps even affected Angryd's life—and the lives of others. Stuff that was buried alive resurfaced, and my closure letter turned out to be the straw that broke the camel's back. Things got out of hand and way too complicated. The best thing to do is let it all go. We need to give up the ghosts of yesteryears and free ourselves from the past.

Ghosts have haunted and taunted us for long enough. Let us come to an end with all of this. It is the perfect time to nail the coffin shut. I know that God is in all of this. His presence surrounds us. There is nowhere to turn, nowhere to run, and nowhere to hide. He will find us—wherever we go. Too many people are involved. As far as I am concerned, everything has unfolded and is fully exposed. My unspoken words have been spoken. All I ever wanted to say has been said. As you may have observed, the first letter of each chapter creates the word truce. We can call a truce and end the cheap drama once and for all. This secret of mine is no longer hidden. It is now exposed. Unashamed and unafraid, I have shared my testimony with you.

All of us exist in different times and realities. We have all grown up, and things can never be the same. I am ready to put this all behind me and move forward. When God's Word starts to probe us, we become uncomfortable—and we discover ourselves and our weaknesses. His words cut deeply into us, separating flesh from spirit. He shows us everything about ourselves—our innermost thoughts and our failures.

When an encounter takes place with God, we get revelations for ourselves and feel the presence of God. The Holy Spirit brings conviction, and we are never the same. Nothing is hidden from God! Everything is uncovered and laid bare before the eyes of God. We must give account to Him. Our behavior, thoughts, and attitudes are all exposed before God. It is such a relief to stop hiding, covering up, and pretending to keep up appearances. The light of Jesus Christ allows us see ourselves as we really are, and His grace helps us in times of need. I have shared my testimony about God's amazing grace in my life.

John Newton wrote "Amazing Grace" after he had fallen deep into sin. God's grace was sufficient for him, and it will be sufficient today—even for Sindi and her sinful state. She has reached the lowest depths of sin. She was living a sin-polluted, corrupted, and conceited life for a long, long time. The Lord—in all His mercy and grace—wants to do the work of transforming her heart. He knows how to do that all by Himself because He is God. I am waiting to hear Sindi sing "Amazing Grace" as the Lord finishes the work He began in her. I believe we all have a song to sing, and no one else can sing yours like you can. I pray that each of us will one day sing and share our songs of God's amazing grace with someone else. I pray that you will receive Jesus Christ as your Lord and Savior.

It is truly amazing what God can do in our lives when we are willing to cooperate with Him. He can bring new life into of any situation. I have chosen to walk by faith and not by sight. God is greater than any work of Satan. I will remain alert and watchful. I do not want to miss any of my God-given opportunities. I have heard that God uses the sin of humanity to bring about His plan for eternity. I could have easily named Sindi Satan in this book, but I chose not to because Sindi was Satan's cohort. He used her to accomplish his purpose of death and destruction.

Sindi continues to stumble in the darkness of sin. We need to flush out internal conflicts of anger, hatred, and unforgiveness from our inner system. If we choose to massage them, we could eventually be destroyed. The Lord does not want us to remain in darkness and error.

The more we choose to indulge in crime and sin, the greater the punishment and anguish we will experience.

Sindi has a chance to make things right with her Maker. Otherwise, she will be facing death, uncertain of her spiritual destiny. God will reveal Himself to Sindi. She will come face-to-face with herself and her sins. She is alone, unhappy, and exhausted. She is a torn-up, overwhelmed woman instead of the superwoman she believes she is. She controlled her life and her family's lives. Now, God is asking her to turn the controls over to Him and surrender all to Him. The script is already written, and the pen is still in His hand. With just one stroke of His pen, Sindi's future can be changed forever.

Satan's reign is over. God has taken back control from Satan and Sindi. I have received God's gift of salvation. This gift is now being offered to Sindi. Will she receive this offer or reject it? The right choice will lead her to eternal life. The wrong choice will lead her to eternal death—where she will endure the penalty for her sins eternally. The choice is hers.

Sindi has an opportunity to make a fresh start before it is too late. The One who came to save us will judge us. Take your seat and position yourself for the climactic end to this redemptive event you are about to witness. This is an ordained, appointed time. In the *Fullness of Time*, heaven meets earth and Jesus meets Sindi. "The time is fulfilled and the kingdom of God is at hand: Repent ye and believe the gospel" (Mark 1:15).

"The Spirit of the Lord is upon me, because He hath anointed me to preach the gospel to the poor. He hath sent me to heal the brokenhearted, to preach deliverance to the captives, and recovering of sight to the blind, to set at liberty them that are bruised. To preach the acceptable year of the Lord" (Luke 4:18–19).

"This day is this scripture fulfilled in your ears" (Luke 4:21).

Since the beginning, certain things have been known to be rivals: God and Satan, good and evil, spirit and flesh, secular and sacred, life and death, light and dark, positive and negative, spiritual and natural, and dogs and cats. It looks like a new item has been added to the list: Sindi and Delight.

In my life, I have observed three things to be true:

- There is a thin line between love and hate.
- There is a thin line between sanity and insanity.
- There is a thin line between life and death.

Sindi has crossed all three of these lines. If we are not careful, she could cause all of us to do the same. The wages of sin is death. If Sindi continues to walk in darkness, it will lead her to total destruction and death. If she chooses to walk in the light of Jesus, she will live and have life. The choice is hers to make. Eternal life is a gift from God.

Power, when carelessly used, can be destructive. Absolute power destroys absolutely. Like Sindi, I have inherited some power by obtaining the title of wife to my husband. I pray I will never have any cause to use this power to shame, humiliate, or disgrace my husband publicly or otherwise. He deserves better! All I have to offer him are respect and love—now and forever. Will this cause me to be loved any more or less? I don't think so. When I receive all the love I am given, I can offer the same to others. Without love, we are empty vessels. The only thing that can bring fullness to an empty vessel is the love of God—and then the love for one another.

I am Princess Delight. I am a daughter of the King. I believe this was all God's agenda. In my wilderness experience, I surrendered myself to God and allowed Him to work in my life as only He could. Forty-one years later, God has enabled me—through His supernatural power—to fulfill His calling for my life. In God's eyes, I was ready, but I was not quite ready in my mind. God used my past and present to place me into my purpose. He knew my heart, and He wanted to resurrect something He placed in my heart a long time ago.

It is now the appointed time. God is my solid rock. After Him are Decell and Oldie. These three individuals know exactly what initiated this ongoing feud with Sindi. She was fighting her own battle until God intervened and said, "Enough is enough." God will accomplish whatever He has set out to do in our lives. His work will be accomplished no matter what!

"Declaring the end from the beginning and from ancient times the things that are not yet done, saying, 'My counsel shall stand, And I will do all My pleasure. Calling a ravenous bird from the east, The man that executeth My counsel, from a far country. Yea, I have spoken it: I will also bring it to pass. I have purposed it; I will also do it'" (Isa. 46:10–11).

I have told the truth, the whole truth, and nothing but the truth. It is my version of the truth. I was not seeking revenge. I did only what I felt was right. In doing so, I was awakened to the ugly workings of evil and its presence. When one stands for truth and for what is right, fingers will be pointed. You cannot fight fire with fire. Error cannot be defeated with error but with truth.

Martin Luther King said, "Darkness cannot put out Darkness, only the light can. Hate cannot destroy hate, only love can."

Fullness of Time has come—all *in His Perfect Time*. As we move closer to the end of our human cycle, may we all try to resolve the chaos and confusion and abound in the work of God. It is the only thing that really matters. God is not a God of confusion but the God of order. I have experienced abuse, lying, misrepresentation, and slander. I did not retaliate until the Holy Spirit prompted me to do so. I am not about to trade truth for truce. My truth has already been told, and all is well with my soul. We each have our own calling. My desire is to do the work of He who sent me—and I want to finish the work. As for me and my house, we will continue to serve the Lord. Jesus is calling you now! Will you run from Him or run to Him? Will you receive the Lord or reject Him? The choice is yours. His grace surrounds us, and it is sufficient. His love is real! If we accept His call, His love will bring us safely into God's house. When Christ leads us to the Cross, He takes us to a place of brokenness, which is necessary for us on our earthly journeys. Our reward will be In His presence—eternally.

I sincerely believe God set up all of this to show us Himself. Only God can make the impossible possible, reverse the curses of the enemies, lead them into their own traps, and bring on their demise. Only God can demonstrate, manifest, reveal, and show Himself and His presence. When He does, nothing can be said about the presence of the Living God.

"It is appointed unto men once to die, but after this the judgment" (Heb. 9:27).

Only God knows the exact circumstance that will bring forth the changes we need. He knows the perfect time, and He will not exceed that time. When He flips the switch—whether we exist in a penthouse or a pigpen, a prison or a palace, a castle or a chicken coop—we will all come face-to-face with Jesus. Life takes us to many unexpected places, but God's love will always bring us home.

I still do not know what the intended game plan was or how it was supposed to be played out. I had no idea what Sindi and Oldie wanted, but I delighted myself in the Lord. He granted me the desires of my heart with His divine intention. God is real, and His grace is sufficient. I can now go and tell it on the mountain over the hills and everywhere that Jesus Christ is Lord. My God is unchanging. He does not change his mind. He is the same yesterday, today, and forever. His promises are all true, and He does just what He says He will do!

Decell and my sons surprised me with an awesome Christmas gift in 2014. They presented me with an iPad. I told them I would put it to good use, and I started writing. In January 2015, as I began writing this book, I turned away from my iPad for a moment. When I returned to my writing, words appeared on the screen: God does not change His mind. He means what He says, and He will do what He says He will do. His plans are brilliant for us the first time when He diligently wrote our stories and thought up every last detail, sequentially numbering the pages of our bios long before we were born, before this day ever came to pass.

These words and sentences were not written or typed by me. It was not part of the material for my book, yet it had perfect relevance to what the book was about. My husband, three of my grandchildren, and I were the only ones at home when it occurred. My husband said he did not write it, and I believe him. The writing was above the level of my grandchildren's abilities. This remains a mystery to my family and me. I am not doubting God's power or His presence. I am in awe. All I can say now is how amazing, brilliant, and magnificent our God is. He is no respecter of persons. He deserves all the glory and all the honor. My eyes have seen the glory of the Lord. In His transcendent glory, He manifested His power, love, and presence to me. My husband and my grandchildren witnessed it. My response is worship, reverence, and awe. The goodness of the Lord is amazing. I hope everyone gets to experience this.

"What the devil meant for evil, God turned it around for good" (Rom. 8:28).

We know that all things work together for good to those who love God. They are called according to His purpose.

Before, during, and after the completion of my book, my faith in God was tested! In this time of testing, my faith in God increased. In His transcendent glory, God showed-up and proved Himself to be real.

Simultaneously, one of my biggest dreams—writing this book—became a reality. One of my biggest fears (testimony for a second book) became real. In the realm of my realities, I received victory. How great is God?

After forty-one years of wilderness experience, *Fullness of Time* has come. I met Oldie in March 1973, sent the closure e-mail in March 2014, and completed the draft for *Fullness of Time* in March 2015.

God deserves all the praise and all the glory. I received my breakthrough at the ordained time set by God. I also received my deliverance at the ultimate moment in time. God gave me this assignment at the right time—the appointed time.

Pastor A. R Bernard said, "Jesus is Lord, period! We believe it, we proclaim it, and we are seeing it come to pass."

May God be with us in our end and in our departing—I ask this and pray in Jesus's name. Amen

Conclusion

It is always a delight to be in God's presence. It is my delight to be with you and share my testimony. Your presence delights me. God made all of this possible. His Son, Jesus, is the true light of the world. The Divine Author has spoken. He has spoken through the writer, and the writer is speaking to the reader: you! I am simply Princess Delight, and I thank you for your time.

In *This Day We Fight,* Pastor Francis Frangipane explained the meaning of *appointed time.*

> For those unaware, an appointed time is, in truth, an open display of the sovereignty and power of God. In it we discover with absolute certainty that nothing is impossible for God. It is a season when God fulfills the hopes and dreams of His people. The Psalmist wrote, But You, O Lord, abide forever, and Your name to all generations. You will arise and have compassion on Zion;

for it is time to be gracious to her, for the appointed time has come (Ps. 102:12–13). During an appointed time it's as though the Lord physically rises and moves in unfailing compassion on behalf of His people. It is the time when divine promises, dreams and spiritual hopes are fulfilled. Recall: Abraham and Sarah had waited in faith for a quarter century for the promise of God. Finally, as they neared one hundred years of age, the Lord told Abraham, At the appointed time I will return to you and Sarah will have a son (Gen. 18:14). One year later, at the appointed time (Gen. 21:2), Isaac was born to aged parents!

I hope this quote helps you to understand the message of *Fullness of Time*. I pray that it brings you truth and clarity regarding God and His perfect time. In 2016, spiritual warfare is still evident. I am happy to report that an entire year has passed without a single word from Sindi by phone or e-mail. Praise God for shutting the mouth of the enemy and silencing the voices of evil.

Looking back at all I encountered over the last two years, I can sum up this book with six songs: Two are for Decell: "One in a Million You" by Larry Graham and "All of Me Loves All of You" by John Legend. Two are for Oldie: "Someone Like You" and "Hello" by Adele. One is for Sindi: "I Started a Joke" by The Bee Gees. That song is about someone who did something horribly wrong, which caused the person to be alienated. The last song is for me: "Lord, I Offer You My Life" by Hillsong.

The promptings of the Holy Spirit made me decide to take the time to write this book. I wrote it so my children, grandchildren, great-grandchildren, and great-great-grandchildren will come to know a part of my life story and my testimony of God. May the Holy Spirit convict them of sin, lead them to confession and repentance—so that they will come to know and receive the Lord as their Savior and taste His goodness. In the end, God will be given all honor and glory.

Lord, I am thankful to you for bringing me to the completion of this book. You are the Perfecter of all, the true Author and Finisher of our faith. I didn't think I had the ability to do this, but trusting in You and believing in You made it all possible. With God, all things are possible. You are truly the Gift-Giver, and I can only say thank you. This book is a testimony of my faith in God. My book may never make the best-seller list, and I may never earn a penny from it, but if it makes an impact on just one person, I will be content. I will be forever grateful for the difference it made in the life of that one person.

This book is one of the most meaningful gifts I could ever give my husband, children, grandchildren, and loved ones. It is a declaration of my faith in God. You have proven yourself to me over and over again. I pray this faith I have in You, Lord, will be transferred to my loved ones as they continue to live in ways that are pleasing to You!

The Alpha and Omega; the first and the last—all glory and honor belong to You!

Printed in the United States
By Bookmasters